DAILY REFLECTIONS FOR LENT 2011

DAILY REFLECTIONS
FOR LENT 2011

VIRGINIA SMITH

ST. ANTHONY MESSENGER PRESS
Cincinnati, Ohio

RESCRIPT

In accord with the *Code of Canon Law,* I hereby grant the *Imprimatur* ("Permission to Publish") to *Daily Reflections for Lent 2011* by Virginia Smith.

Reverend Joseph R. Binzer
Vicar General
Archdiocese of Cincinnati
Cincinnati, Ohio
September 7, 2010

The *Imprimatur* ("Permission to Publish") is a declaration that a book or pamphlet is considered to be free of doctrinal or moral error. It is not implied that those who have granted the *Imprimatur* agree with the contents, opinions or statements expressed.

Cover and book design by Mark Sullivan
Cover image copyright © Jaroslaw Grudzinski l Dreamstime.com

ISBN 978-0-86716-992-8

Published by St. Anthony Messenger Press
28 W. Liberty St.
Cincinnati, OH 45202
www.AmericanCatholic.org
www.SAMPBooks.org

Printed in the United States of America.

Printed on acid-free paper.

11 12 13 14 15 5 4 3 2 1

· · · | · · ·
Introduction

What seems most important to you this Lent? Where would you like these next forty days to take you on your journey to Easter?

Reflect on this and then put the entire endeavor in God's hands, realizing that God's plans for your Lent may differ considerably from your own. As one priest I know recommends, try focusing on one particular area of spiritual growth each Lent rather than a broad spectrum.

The church's slant on the season is contained succinctly in Preface I of Lent: "Each year you [God] give us this joyful season when we prepare to celebrate the paschal mystery with mind and heart renewed." Joy? That's the last emotion many people associate with Lent.

In these pages let's attempt to rediscover lenten joy as well as take a barefaced look at ourselves and our lives. That may seem like an oxymoron, but such clear-eyed introspection is intended to reveal the good in our lives as well as areas that need work. Scripture readings for the day's Mass lay the groundwork, with the reflection that follows expanding on one or another of those scriptural themes. Finally, a question or action and a short prayer are designed to spur further meditation.

Adjust any of these components depending on the amount of time you have or how God uses your time together. If a single line in one of the day's readings or in the reflection itself really speaks to you, let its implications soak into your heart and soul. Use this booklet in a personal way, yet remember that no prayer is totally personal: There is always a communal aspect. During Lent, when prayer tends to be more introspective, we want to include others, from those dearest to our hearts to the universal church and the cares of the wider world.

This Lent keep in mind that the most significant words in the Christian vocabulary are, "Alleluia! The Lord is risen!" May we find ourselves singing them loud and clear on Easter.

· · · | · · ·
The Mystery of Ash Wednesday
March 9 • Ash Wednesday
JOEL 2:12–18; 2 CORINTHIANS 5:20—6:2; MATTHEW 6:1–6, 16–18

Churches across the land are crowded today. The question is why. Ash Wednesday is not a holy day of obligation in the United States, and truthfully, holy days generally draw far fewer people. So what is the attraction of Ash Wednesday? Why does it seem to resonate so strongly in the Catholic soul? There are probably a good many answers.

A smudge of ashes on our foreheads contains no magic, but like many Christian symbols, it's intended to remind us of something. Ashes are mentioned over fifty times in the Bible, almost always in the context of repentance or mourning, emotions which were also frequently accompanied by the tearing of garments. The prophet Joel tells the people of his day, "…rend your hearts and not your clothing." Many come before the Lord on Ash Wednesday to do just that.

Others may see Ash Wednesday as a kind of spiritual New Year, a time to make resolutions, to wipe the old slate clean and begin again. Still others seek a more intimate connection with God. And some could not tell you why they search out a church on Ash Wednesday; it just seems like the place to be. For these reasons and others we'll never know, today marks the beginning of a great journey whose destination is Easter, the most joyous day of the Christian year.

Reflect
What does Ash Wednesday mean to you? How does it set the tone for the lenten weeks that stretch ahead? What are your hopes for this Lent?

Pray
Repeat the prophet Joel's counsel:

> Return to the LORD, your God,
>   for he is gracious and merciful,
> slow to anger, and abounding in steadfast love.

• • • | • • •

Choose Life!
March 10 • Thursday After Ash Wednesday
DEUTERONOMY 30:15–20; LUKE 9:22–25

Moses would probably be greatly surprised to find his words, "Choose life…," plastered on twenty-first–century bumper stickers, and yet those two short words may be more applicable today than at any other point in human history. Ours has been described as a culture of death which, of course, is totally unacceptable to Christians who see a bright light radiating from an empty tomb on Easter morning.

While much of the world believes in a life-death continuum, Christians have faith in life-death-LIFE. Life once created is never destroyed. Ours is not merely an earthly existence, but an eternal life with a loving God. How can we not rejoice! Although during Lent we mute our alleluias, they should always be there whispering blissfully in the back of our minds.

Luke's Gospel passage today seems to throw cold water on any alleluias with Jesus' talk of his rejection, suffering, and death. But we must not miss the end of the sentence, "…and on the third day be raised." For us, death never has the last word; life always does. As disciples, we follow where Jesus leads, and he takes us right through death to eternal life. And so we choose life in all its forms from conception to natural death, remembering it is the most precious gift of all. Moses knew that; so do we.

Reflect

Do you ever think of death as simply a filmy veil through which we pass to continue in God's eternal realm the life we began here? Spend a little time listening to what God may have to say about that.

Pray

This Lent, O Lord, help me to cleanse myself of the faults and failings I endure in this life as I prepare for eternal life in your heavenly kingdom.

• • • | • • •

Christians, Do Not Report to Central Casting!

March 11 • Friday After Ash Wednesday
ISAIAH 58:1–9A; MATTHEW 9:14–15

No wonder prophets failed to win popularity contests. Isaiah conveys the words of the Lord in such a manner that any audience would be taken aback. This is Third Isaiah, speaking to Israelites newly returned from the Babylonian Exile and striving to start anew. It would be consoling to believe that his words were intended for God's people then and have no relevance today. Unfortunately, that is not the case.

What Isaiah is railing against is the same thing Jesus speaks of many times as well—hypocrisy, a word that literally means "actor." What God seeks in his people of every time and place is sincerity. As Isaiah clearly points out, God isn't against liturgical worship per se, only that which is largely for show and lacks heart. Nor does he oppose fasting and other forms of penitence providing the intention behind them is genuine. In other words, it's not so much *what* we do as *why* we do it.

I know people whose unique worship gestures or practices I find interesting enough to ask about. After receiving the sacred Host, one friend always lifts her cupped hands high before consuming it. When asked why, she said it was a sign of adoration. For her, it's tremendously meaningful and powerful. That, I believe, is the attitude God looks for in our relationship with him. Actors need not apply.

Reflect

What areas of personal or communal devotion are most meaningful to you? The Sign of the Cross? Holy water? The Eucharist? Why? Does something truly unique have special significance for you?

Pray

May every thought, every word, every gesture of my relationship with you overflow with earnestness and authenticity, O Lord. Teach me to be ever more attentive to the most treasured relationship in my life.

• • • | • • •

God's Love for His People
March 12 • Saturday After Ash Wednesday
Isaiah 58:9b–14; Luke 5:27–32

Today's reading from Isaiah immediately follows yesterday's. If God's words spoken through the prophet seemed harsh yesterday, a totally different tone prevails today. You might find it profitable to read both passages together to get a real sense of the contrast. Yesterday, God thundered against mere lip service. Today, he continues, "If you…," and goes on to list the qualities in his followers that win his approval. For the most part, these are what we would call social justice issues today: removing the yoke, feeding the hungry, satisfying the needs of the afflicted.

Almsgiving has long been one of the pillars of lenten observance. Even if money is tight and immovable obligations many, there is always the possibility of donating time or talent. Time is perhaps our most valuable commodity, and its gift would not go unnoticed by a loving God. Your parish may well have projects for which it needs volunteers. Your special talents, gifts from God, may be just what are needed.

However you decide to give, merely focusing on the broader community and those whose wants are greater than your own will make a worthwhile lenten practice.

Reflect

Should you decide to help fund specific projects, how do you choose from the glut of requests that crowd your mailbox? Most are worthy, but to which does God seem to be calling you? Should you give all you have available to one charity or a little to several? As a good steward, it is wise to give that some thought.

Pray

My God, you have been so generous in your gifts to me. Guide my judgment as I attempt to share those gifts prudently with those suffering hardship locally, nationally, and internationally.

New Beginnings

March 13 • First Sunday of Lent
GENESIS 2:7–9; 3:1–7; ROMANS 5:12–19; MATTHEW 4:1–11

Although Sundays are not included in the season of Lent because every Sunday is considered a little Easter, today's readings have a lenten tone. They're all about fresh starts. In Genesis, the first man and woman are created and then stumble badly. In Romans, Jesus, seen as a second Adam, comes to reverse that stumble. "Oh, happy fault," as we shall hear in the Exsultet at the Easter Vigil; happy because without it, we would have had no need of the presence among us of the Son of God. Matthew speaks of Jesus' desert temptation, a prelude to the opening of his public ministry. Clearly, we are intended to grasp something about new beginnings here.

Life is full of pristine moments for most of us. Some are sought. Others are foisted upon us by circumstance. Graduations, weddings, new jobs, and new communities are all opportunities for beginning again in everyday life.

In the spiritual life, Catholicism offers a rather unique opening to an unsullied relationship with God in the sacrament of reconciliation. Once it was best known as confession, but that term was not entirely accurate. There's more to it than that. Then we began to hear of "penance services"—a term which also fails to provide the complete picture. Confession and penitence are certainly components of the sacrament, but the key lies in reconciliation—a new beginning, a fresh start with God. We need not drag our past sins like lead weights around our ankles through the remainder of our lives. God graciously allows us to begin anew each time the priest absolves us. What a gift! But a gift, sad to say, that is seldom taken advantage of these days.

Reflect
Many parishes offer communal penance services during Lent. How wonderful it would be if the churches were packed by those seeking a new beginning with God. Resolve to be among that number in your own parish.

Pray
Lord, there is no sin too great for your gracious mercy to wipe away. Let me remember that I have up to and including my last conscious breath to make a fresh start with you.

• • • | • • •

What Does It Mean to Be Holy?

March 14 • First Monday of Lent
LEVITICUS 19:1–2, 11–18; MATTHEW 25:31–46

What synonym would you use for the word *holy? Saintly,*
perhaps? It's certainly a possibility, but if we throw that
word out there, it will boomerang right back and land in
our laps, for all of us are called to be saints. It's the primary vocation of every Christian.

Today's reading from Leviticus is part of what is often
called the Holiness Code (chapters 17–26). You may be
surprised to find elements of the Decalogue (Ten
Commandments) there in addition to admonitions that
you thought were introduced by Jesus—for instance,
"…but you shall love your neighbor as yourself." It helps
to remember that Jesus was an observant Jew, thoroughly steeped in the teachings of the Hebrew
Scriptures. In Luke chapter 10, a lawyer asks Jesus what
he must do to gain eternal life. Jesus asks, "What is written in the law? What do you read there?" The lawyer
answers, "You shall love the Lord your God with all your
heart, and with all your soul and with all your strength,
and with all your mind; and your neighbor as yourself"

(verse 27). Jesus approves his answer, and there may be no better definition of holiness anywhere. Then, when asked for an example, Jesus tells the parable of the Good Samaritan.

Notice that the focus in both of today's readings is primarily on our relationship with one another. Only Matthew tells the story of the sheep and the goats, again demonstrating, as he often does, how to bring about the kingdom of God on earth, and telling us that holiness is found in how we live our lives every day. It's not just for canonized saints, but for us, the saints in training.

Reflect
Would you be embarrassed if someone called you holy or said, "Good morning, Saint [insert your name here]"? Why would that make you uncomfortable?

Pray
If I am to be yours in time and eternity, O God, holiness must be my goal. Show me how to live a holy life in my particular circumstances, to love you above all and my neighbor as myself.

· · · | · · ·

"Pray Then in This Way…"

March 15 • First Tuesday of Lent
ISAIAH 55:10–11; MATTHEW 6:7–15

Last Saturday we spoke of almsgiving as one of the long-standing pillars of lenten observance. Today's Gospel reading from the Sermon on the Mount brings us to a second, prayer. Only one other version of this particular prayer is contained in the Gospels, in Luke 11:2–4. It is thought-provoking to compare the similarities and differences.

Matthew's rendering begins with an invocation, followed by three appeals relating to the glory of God, then our own petitions. God is always first. What has come to be known as the Lord's Prayer is compact in verbiage, yet says so much. I think of that in relation to my own prayer which sometimes seems to rattle on endlessly. Still we are told to "Pray in the Spirit at all times…" (Ephesians 6:18a). How do we reconcile the two approaches?

We might begin by recalling that not all prayer is vocal or verbal. A man spent a couple of hours each day in his parish church. When asked what he said to God all that time, he gently replied, "Oh, not much. I look at God, and God looks at me." That kind of contemplative prayer has been a staple of devout Christian life for many centuries.

Short prayers during our busy day, three or four words, also help keep our focus on God. "Lord, help me." "Holy Spirit, grant me wisdom." "Thank you, Jesus." Once the habit has been formed, these come almost as second nature.

Variety adds yet another dimension. The four traditional forms of prayer are praise, petition, penitence, and thanksgiving. But whatever style you choose, the most important thing is simply to pray.

Reflect

No one type of prayer is ideal all the time. At various times of our lives, one form may be more useful than another. Try a prayer style that is new to you, and you may find it rejuvenates your relationship with God.

Pray

The apostles asked Jesus to teach them to pray. I echo their prayer, Lord, in the hope that it will result in a closer, deeper rapport with you.

How Do We Recognize God in Our Lives?

March 16 • First Wednesday of Lent
JONAH 3:1–10; LUKE 11:29–32

Remember how we talked last week about ashes as an ancient expression of repentance? Today's reading from Jonah provides a perfect example. The king of Nineveh and his people believe the prophet Jonah and promptly do penance, an incredible accomplishment pointed to by Jesus in Luke. We moderns may fail to get the bite of the story inasmuch as today's portion neglects to mention that Nineveh was the capital of the feared and despised Assyrians who had hauled the ten northern tribes of Israel into captivity several centuries earlier. Jesus' point is that even this personification of evil recognized the Word of God when they heard it, and he is troubled by his own audience's constant requests for a sign to prove he really comes from God.

An American man, so the story goes, was warned by a firefighter to leave his home because of rising floodwaters. He refused, saying, "God will protect me." As the waters rose, a boat came past offering him safe passage. Again, he replied, "God will protect me." Finally, forced to his roof, he saw a helicopter hovering and lowering a ladder, but he waved them off as well. Ultimately, the man drowned. Arriving before God, he said, "Why didn't you protect me?" To which God responded, "I sent you a warning, a boat, and a helicopter. What more did you want?"

God arrives in our lives every day, but on his own terms. If we, like the man in the story, have preconceived ideas of how God's presence will appear, we're very likely to miss him altogether.

Reflect
Have I already decided how God will come into my life in various sets of circumstances? Could I be more open to a constantly surprising God?

Pray
Jesus, let me take to heart your words to the people of your time. Help me to recognize you in places that never occurred to me before.

$\bullet \ \bullet \ \bullet \ | \ \bullet \ \bullet \ \bullet$

What Do We Expect to Happen When We Pray?

March 17 • First Thursday of Lent
ESTHER C:12, 14–16, 23–25; MATTHEW 7:7–12

Queen Esther is in a real dilemma in today's First Reading. She realizes she has almost no influence at all, both because she is a woman and because she is a foreigner married to the powerful Persian king. But she also knows that, if the Israelite people living in that empire have any hope of survival, it's up to her. Her prayer to God is earnest, fervent, even desperate. But clearly she has every expectation that God will not only hear her, but act.

In the Gospel reading, Jesus makes it clear that Esther had a right to assume God's response. "Ask, and it will be given you…". Since prayer is an essential component of lenten observance, this may be a good time to ask ourselves what we really expect to happen when we pray. This is where faith comes in—faith in the power of God, faith in the promises of Jesus. Our part is simply to believe.

We can, of course, make the mistake of thinking that our prayers will be answered exactly as we have stated in our requests, forgetting that God sees the big picture, not merely our small part in it. If what we've asked for is not in our own interests or that of others, it may be reframed into a larger context. While we are gazing straight down the street looking for the answer we prayed for, another better answer may be coming around the corner behind us. Often it's easier to see God's action in retrospect. Looking back on a situation, it becomes apparent that God was working to our benefit. When I lost a job years ago, it seemed like the end of my world. From my vantage point today, I can see it was the best thing that ever happened to me. "Ask, and it will be given you…"—as God sees fit.

Reflect
Do you sincerely believe that God will act when you pray? Can you recall a time in your life when a prayer was answered very differently than you envisioned?

Pray
Strengthen my faith, O Lord, that you hear and answer my prayers. Open the eyes of my soul to see your love when those prayers are answered another way.

· · · | · · ·
Defining Righteousness
March 18 • First Friday of Lent
Ezekiel 18:21–28; Matthew 5:20–26

Both of today's readings speak of righteousness. In fact, it is a major theme in the Gospel of Matthew. But inasmuch as it is not a word that comes up regularly in everyday conversation, what exactly does it mean? It can be defined as "wisdom" or "prudence," qualities certainly that all of us should strive to possess. However, in a Judeo-Christian context, there's rather more to it. To be righteous is to be godly, not perfect by any means, but devout in our efforts to live the laws of God.

A few verses prior to today's reading, Jesus says, "Do not think that I have come to abolish the law or the prophets. I have come not to abolish but to fulfill." In doing so, he takes admonitions from the heart of the Mosaic Law, the Decalogue, and expands them. In this extract from the Sermon on the Mount, he tells his audience that there's more to the commandment against killing than previously thought. People can be murdered by rash words as easily as by the sword. What was good enough twelve hundred years before his time needs to be developed and deepened. If that was true in Jesus' day, what does it say about our own? Should more not be expected of us?

Ezekiel, speaking for God, says, "…for the righteousness that they have done they shall live. Have I any pleasure in the death of the wicked?" God, whether of the Old Testament or the New, is a loving God who is always on our side. Nonetheless, we are required to do our part. Lent is a particularly good time to give that some thought.

Reflect

If Jesus gave the Sermon on the Mount today, what issues would he lay before us that didn't even exist in his day? Legalized abortion? Weapons of mass destruction? Genocide?

Pray

I may not be able to effect much change on the world stage, O Lord, but I can be more life-affirming in all I do. As to Jesus' warning about killing others with my words, let me remember the Letter of James, "How great a forest is set ablaze by a small fire. And the tongue is a fire" (3:5b–6a).

· · · | · · ·

The Man We Know So Little and Revere So Much

March 19 • First Saturday of Lent
Solemnity of Saint Joseph
2 SAMUEL 7:4-5A, 12-14A; ROMANS 4:13, 16-18, 22;
MATTHEW 1:16, 18-21, 24A; OR LUKE 2:41-51A

The Gospels tell us little about Jesus' foster father. Most of what we know about Joseph is contained in the first two chapters of Matthew and the second chapter of Luke. Mark never mentions him at all. He is thought to have died before Jesus' public ministry began as we hear nothing of him during those years. For that reason, he has been named the patron of a happy death, presuming that he died with Jesus and Mary at his side. The church devotes the entire month of March to Joseph, and, of course, today we venerate him especially in a great solemnity, Catholicism's highest-ranking observance. And the church itself is dedicated in a very special way to Joseph.

What merits all this attention when factual information is so sparse? Primarily Joseph's great faith. This humble man from a backwater in Galilee was totally unprepared for the role he was to play. And Mary's explanation probably didn't help much, as she was equally bewildered by the situation into which Joseph was inextricably drawn. That he was a kind man is clear from his reluctance to expose Mary to public humiliation, knowing that it could easily result in stoning. That he was a strong man is equally apparent in that he squared his shoulders and went about doing what he believed God wanted of him, however little he understood it. In every sense of the word, Joseph was a gentle man. We only wish we knew him better.

Reflect

Gentleness, humility, strength, obedience, and faith are qualities we all seek. The church has long held Joseph up as a model for us to emulate. Perhaps that's what was intended by placing his feast day during March so it always falls during Lent.

Pray

Dear Saint Joseph, so humble on earth, so honored in heaven, pray for me that I may learn from you the qualities which so endeared you to Jesus and his Mother and emulate those virtues as best I can.

. . . | . . .

Past, Present, and Future

March 20 • Second Sunday of Lent

Genesis 12:1–4a; 2 Timothy 1:8b–10; Matthew 17:1–9

The official celebration of the Transfiguration each year falls on August 6, so it seems a bit odd to encounter it on a lenten Sunday. What is the rationale behind that, I wonder? Not being a liturgist by trade, I can't say with any certainty, but looking at all three of today's readings in juxtaposition, one idea does emerge. Perhaps these passages are intended to remind us that the inexorable march to the cross that holds our focus during these penitential weeks is neither the beginning nor the end for the Christ.

In Genesis, we hear of the promise to Abram, an assurance of "a great nation." As the first verifiably historical figure in Scripture, Abram/Abraham opens the never-ending chapter of God's personal relationship with a chosen people.

Second Timothy maintains that this was not the beginning at all: "This grace was given to us in Christ Jesus before the ages began." Long before there were such a people, long before there was anything material at all, there was Christ.

And, as the Transfiguration suggests, long after creation as we know it is a distant memory, there will still be Christ...and us. Jesus' entire ministry points to our eternal future in the realm of a loving God.

Where, then, do the messages of these three readings lead? For me, they point to hope, the beginnings of the Judeo-Christian tradition with Abram; the affirmation of Jesus' eternal divinity in Timothy; and the assurance of life everlasting with the same Jesus, the Christ, in the kingdom of his Father. What an inconceivable future is ours!

Reflect

If you were to see the transfigured Jesus suddenly standing in front of you as the apostles did, how do you think you might react? The Gospel says Peter, James, and John responded in fear, but in an instance such as this, that, no doubt, really means awe. What would you say to this breathtaking presence?

Pray

Remind me often, Jesus, that the cross is not the end of your story—that there is no end to your story...or mine.

⋯ | ⋯

Do Not Judge But Forgive
March 21 • Second Monday of Lent
DANIEL 9:4B–10; LUKE 6:36–38

A woman who had suffered much in a Nazi labor camp during World War II survived with hatred in her heart for her captors and a strong desire for revenge. Some years after the war, while standing on the platform at a railway station, she chanced to see one of her guards chatting with friends nearby. After watching him for several minutes, it occurred to her that her vengeful heart wasn't hurting him one bit, but it was eating her alive. Mustering what must have taken a great deal of courage, she walked over, tapped him on the shoulder, and introduced herself. He visibly paled. But holding out her hand, she quietly said, "I just want you to know that I forgive you." What a lesson for us all!

Jesus' insistence that we forgive is not to see if we can actually do something tremendously difficult. Like all his expectations, this one is for our own good. Grudges and resentments can take over our whole lives, making it difficult or even impossible to move on in our spiritual lives.

Then, too, we are actually incapable of judging others. We cannot even judge ourselves with any degree of accuracy. No matter how old we get, we continue to be surprised, or worse yet shocked, by some of the things we think, say, or do. What was the motivation of the Nazi guard? Was he somehow forced into his position? The inmate couldn't ever know, so forgiveness was the only option.

Reflect

Have you ever been hurt by a person who misjudged you badly? Do you think you may have done the same thing to someone else?

Pray

Make it clear to me when I am being judgmental, O Lord, and give me the courage to seek forgiveness when I have wronged my sister or brother.

• • • | • • •

The Prophets Weigh In

March 22 • Second Tuesday of Lent
Isaiah 1:10, 16–20; Matthew 23:1–12

If you've been looking for some readings with a real penitential flair, this is the week for you. Yesterday, we heard from Daniel. Today, Isaiah has some tough words for us. Tomorrow and Thursday, he will yield the floor to Jeremiah. And Micah will round out the week on Saturday. Remembering that these men lived at different times and under different conditions, it's a little surprising how similar their messages are.

But, on second thought, maybe not. The basic point all of them made to God's people was: You've got to change direction. You're wandering away from God and the covenant you made with him.

There's not much question that the reason we hear so much from the prophets during Lent is that we need to heed their words every bit as much as our ancestors did. Human nature wasn't perfect then and isn't perfect now. We tend to become complacent, to think that the status quo is good enough. The prophets were sent to shake the Israelites out of their lethargy. For that reason alone, they won no popularity contests. In fact, a little of everything was tried in an attempt to shut them up: exile, imprisonment, even murder. One hopes that we don't go to such extremes now, but it could be that we would benefit from listening more attentively to the prophetic voices of the early twenty-first century.

Reflect

When you think of contemporary prophetic voices, what names cross your mind? Is that primarily because you agree with them? Are there other voices you aren't so keen to listen to that might deserve a hearing?

Pray

I know that prophets are not confined to the biblical era. Help me, Holy Spirit of all wisdom, to discern those I should listen to attentively today.

• • • | • • •

Yet Another Failure to Listen

March 23 • Second Wednesday of Lent
JEREMIAH 18:18–20; MATTHEW 20:17–28

Yesterday we talked about the prophets' difficulty getting people to listen. Today, Jeremiah and Jesus have the same problem. Jeremiah, who preaches loud and long trying to save the Judahites from the threat of exile to Babylon, receives nothing but abuse for his efforts. The only thanks he gets are plots against his life. The thinking goes something like this: "Let's get rid of him. No one will miss him. He's just annoying." The prophet turns to his God, asking in effect what he's doing wrong to merit such a response. The answer, of course, is nothing.

Even more shocking is the response to Jesus' prediction of his impending horrific suffering, death, and resurrection. Taking the twelve aside, he speaks to them very clearly about his imminent fate. Later, the mother of James and John—who presumably had not heard Jesus' remarks—asks for preferential treatment for her sons. The other ten apostles become irate, not that the subject should be raised at such a sensitive time, but that they weren't in on vying for position. No wonder they were incredulous about Jesus' Resurrection that first Easter. They weren't listening when he specifically told them of the greatest event in human history.

When I hear the Scripture readings at Mass, it sometimes seems as though I've never heard a particular passage before, although I must have encountered it dozens of times. Obviously, I wasn't paying attention either. If all we do this Lent is hone our listening skills, it may turn out to be a very profitable time for us.

Reflect
Choose a biblical passage, possibly one of today's readings, and spend some time with it. Pore carefully over

what is being said and what the implications of that may be. Really listen to it.

Pray

Too often, Lord, when I think I am praying, I am really allowing my mind to wander in all directions. How can I hope to hear you through the din of my own distractions? Help me better listen to you.

• • • | • • •

The Beggar at the Door

March 24 • Second Thursday of Lent
JEREMIAH 17:5–10; LUKE 16:19–31

Luke records parables of Jesus that are chronicled in no other Gospel: the Good Samaritan, the Prodigal Son, and today, the Rich Man and Lazarus. First, note that this Lazarus is fictional, not to be confused with the man Jesus raises from the dead in the eleventh chapter of John. The contrast between the two protagonists in this story couldn't have been greater. The rich man, sometimes called Dives, has everything; Lazarus has nothing. The two probably saw each other every day, but that is where it ended. As far as we know, the rich man never abused Lazarus; he simply ignored him.

Lazarus may have become something like a dog I once owned who loved to curl up at a certain spot on the carpet because the sun shone there and it was warm. She slept there so often that I automatically raised my foot in passing in order not to step on her, even when she was nowhere in sight. I just didn't think about it.

Nobel Peace Prize laureate and Holocaust survivor Elie Wiesel once commented that the opposite of love is not hate, but indifference. As today's story plays out, we learn the result of the rich man's actions or lack thereof. He will live forever with the choices he made in life, rather like Jacob Marley's ghost in Dickens's *A Christmas Carol*. We will live eternally with our own choices as well. Lent is a very good time to examine our preferences and decisions to see if we would be able to live with them perpetually.

Reflect

The church has long taught that there are sins of omission as well as those of commission, things we ought to do but don't. Sometimes those are intentional; but like the rich man we more often simply put them out of our minds. Do some of yours come to mind?

Pray

Father, let me not go through life blind to the needs of others. Awaken me to the beggar at my door—whoever that may be.

• • • | • • •

Events That Change Lives or Change the World

March 25 • Second Friday of Lent
Solemnity of the Annunciation
Isaiah 7:8-10, 10-14, Hebrews 10:4-10; Luke 1:26-38

All of us experience events that forever change our lives: graduations, weddings, relocations. But perhaps nothing brings about greater or more lasting change than the birth of a child. Today, precisely nine months before we celebrate his birth, we commemorate the conception of the child who changed everything for everyone for all time. The Annunciation to Mary that she would be the vehicle through whom God would become man is chapter one in a Jesus story that has no end. And it all happened in the sleepy little rural community of Nazareth to a village girl barely in her teens.

Did Mary grasp the significance of that day unique in all human history? Not even slightly. She says so herself, "How can this be…?" And yet she accepts that which she cannot grasp, "May it be done to me according to your word." On the Solemnity of Saint Joseph earlier this month, we spoke of his remarkable faith. Here we witness his female counterpart. Mary's trust that whatever God has in mind for her will be in her best interests is noteworthy, especially in one so young and unsophisticated. Only years later will she realize how her innocent profession of faith has come to define her.

When we face a major crossroads in our own lives, we often don't comprehend it any better than that long-ago Nazareth girl. Certainly, we are not given the ability to see its consequences during the years ahead. Like Mary, all we can do is trust God, believing that whatever lies before us will ultimately be in our best interests.

Reflect

We are accustomed to taking biblical events at face value because they are familiar to us. Try putting yourself in Mary's place during the angelic annunciation. How do you think you would react? Why?

Pray

Mary, pray that I may be given the type of faith that characterized your whole life, not only at the annunciation but throughout Jesus' life, public ministry, agony, death, and resurrection.

• • • | • • •

The Forgiving Father

March 26 • Second Saturday of Lent
Micah 7:14–15, 18–20; Luke 15:1–3, 11–32

The parable of the Prodigal Son is very familiar, perhaps too familiar. We may hear, "There was a man who had two sons," and at least subconsciously think, "Oh, that one," and let our mind wander for the remainder of the Gospel. During this lenten season when we try to focus a bit more on matters scriptural, we could benefit from taking a closer look at this old favorite.

First, there's the matter of the title. Luke, of course, placed no labels on his parables. We did that for our own convenience and, in this case, we may have put the accent on the wrong syllable. The primary character is not the Prodigal Son, who may stand for each of us at some point in our lives, but rather the father who, of course, is meant to remind us of God. And it is the character of the father that determines the outcome of the story.

The crucial line is, "But while he [the son] was still far off, his father saw him and was filled with compassion; he ran and put his arms around him and kissed him" (Luke 15:20). Before the young man can blurt out his prepared act of contrition (whether sincere or insincere we never really know), his father is planning a homecoming party. If the father began to run toward the boy the minute he came in sight, he must have been watching for him for days, weeks, months—maybe years.

That's how much God loves each of us. No matter where we've been or what we've done, he is waiting for us, watching for us, yearning for us. Like the Prodigal, we will not be met with stern condemnation, but loving arms and kisses. Hard to believe, but it's true.

Reflect

So many have an image of a harsh, unforgiving God, and that's very sad in light of the devoted Father the Bible describes for us in both testaments. How do you envision your first meeting with God when you move from this life to the next?

Pray

Remind me often that "Father" is not merely the name Jesus said we could call you but a literal description of your role in my life. Let me place my hand in yours with the certain knowledge that the only place you will lead me is home.

• • • | • • •

Coming to Know Who Jesus Really Is

March 27 • Third Sunday of Lent
EXODUS 17:3–7; ROMANS 5:1–2, 5–8; JOHN 4:5–42

For the next three Sundays, we will hear episodes in Jesus' life exclusive to the Gospel of John. As we do, it may be useful to remember that much of John's writing contains multiple layers of meaning or progressions. For example, there is the manner in which the Samaritan woman addresses Jesus. She begins by calling him "a Jew" (verse 9b). Shortly thereafter, she refers to him as "Sir" (verses 11a and 15a). Later, she acknowledges, "I see that you are a prophet" (verse 19b). When she cautiously ventures that she knows a Messiah is coming, Jesus responds, "I am he, the one who is speaking to you" (verse 26).

That's all very interesting, but what does it have to do with us? In John's Gospel, people are frequently found moving closer to or farther from the light. The light, of course, is Jesus himself. This person who, by her own admission, has two strikes against her from the outset (she is a Samaritan despised by Jews and also a woman) comes ever so gradually into the light. For many of us, our faith experience is much the same. Over the years, we come progressively nearer the light of God, and upon occasion stumble backward toward the darkness.

Jesus' discussion with the Samaritan woman is the longest theological dialogue recorded with any individual in the Gospels. If Jesus is so willing to expend his time and energy on a person most of his disciples would see as an outcast unworthy of his notice, we see that in reality there are no outsiders. Jesus will go to unheard-of lengths for any one of us. There isn't a designation splendid enough for that.

Reflect

We can easily see how our human relationships evolve and change over time. Looking back, how do you see your relationship with Jesus growing and expanding?

Pray

The Samaritan woman met Jesus at about noon, the hour when the light is brightest and fullest upon our world. Lord, keep my footsteps moving progressively closer to that light that one day I may step through that gossamer film called death into your everlasting light.

• • • | • • •

About Misunderstandings and Aliens
March 28 • Third Monday of Lent
2 KINGS 5:1–15B; LUKE 4:24–30

Being misunderstood is never fun, and when the disagreement involves those closest to us, it's especially hurtful. In today's Gospel, Jesus has just delivered what amounts to his inaugural address to a hometown audience. In it, he has described his mission, told his friends and family what they can expect from him henceforth. Talking among themselves, Jesus' neighbors and relatives at first applaud his words, and then begin to question them. It's the old "Who does he think he is?" syndrome. And to make a bad matter worse, Jesus defends himself by citing episodes from the Hebrew Scriptures (one of which constitutes today's First Reading) where aliens, outsiders, and foreigners seem to have been favored over God's chosen people. The upshot is that his listeners try to throw him off a cliff.

Jesus, as human as we are, had to be wounded by all of this, but all we are told is, "But he passed through the midst of them and went on his way" (Luke 4:30). He made no attempt to justify himself. He gave no hot, angry response. There's a lesson there for all of us. When we are misjudged, especially by those whose opinion means something to us, the best thing to do is nothing. As the saying goes, the truth will out. Our lives, like Jesus', are our greatest defense.

Also we see in Jesus' mention of the woman in Sidon and Naaman the Syrian that there are no aliens, outsiders, or foreigners in the kingdom of God. All are not merely accepted, but most welcome.

Reflect

Can you think of a time you were seriously misjudged by someone close to you? Of course you were hurt, but how did you react?

Pray

When I am misjudged, my God, I grasp more clearly why you are so emphatic in telling me not to judge another. I am entirely incapable of doing so. Let me also bear in mind that you have said that I will be judged by the same standard I use to judge others.

To Infinity and Beyond

March 29 • Third Tuesday of Lent
Daniel 3:25, 34–43; Matthew 18:21–35

We could scarcely fail to notice the emphasis on forgiveness in the readings for the early weeks of Lent, culminating with the parable of the Forgiving Father (Prodigal Son) last Saturday. Today's Gospel again places that motif center stage, not in a parable, but in a very real episode from Jesus' life.

Peter may be a little tired of it all and wants to get down to real life when he asks, "…how often should I forgive? As many as seven times?" Seven, in Peter's world, was the perfect number. No one could be required to do more than that. Rather than respond with exasperation to his beloved, if grumpy, friend, Jesus uses humor to make his point. There had to be a wry smile on his face as he replied, "Not seven times, but, I tell you, seventy-seven times." Astronomical! Impossible!

But Jesus wasn't kidding, any more than he was when he taught his own prayer which included the daunting line, "And forgive us our debts, / as we also have forgiven our debtors." I always stumble a little over those words. I'm actually inviting God to forgive me in precisely the same manner that I forgive others. Am I ready to say that with complete sincerity? I need to stop and think about that…a lot.

It goes without saying that none of us will ever be able to forgive as God forgives, but Jesus' cryptic remark to Peter tells us to try, try, and try again.

Reflect

Forgiveness is not an emotion, but rather an act of the will, one that may need to be renewed on a daily basis for some time before we sense it has really taken hold. That's useful to remember as we begin any exercise in forgiveness.

Pray

Holy Spirit, bring to my mind whatever and whoever in my life stands in need of my forgiveness. Prompt me also to recall those whose forgiveness I should seek.

• • • | • • •

Not to Abolish But to Fulfill

March 30 • Third Wednesday of Lent
DEUTERONOMY 4:1, 5–9; MATTHEW 5:17–19

In today's excerpt from the Sermon on the Mount, Jesus is about to teach an expanded version of some of the sacrosanct Ten Commandments. Before he does, however, he is careful to reassure his audience, "Do not think that I have come to abolish the law or the prophets; I have come not to abolish but to fulfill" (Matthew 5:17). They should not fear change.

If any people know about change, it is those of us living in the early twenty-first century. Barely a day goes by that we don't see or hear of something that will change our lives for better or worse. For the people of Jesus' day, change was even more threatening. Their lives were governed by Mosaic Law from the time they opened their eyes in the morning until they closed them at night, for secular and religious law were a single unit. To change anything about the Law given to them by God was tantamount to sacrilege. Who, after all, could speak for God or alter in any way what God had commanded?

For Matthew, the answer was clear: God alone could amend God's law. Hence, Jesus was divine. This may seem a little mystifying to us, but Matthew's Jewish audience would understand the allusion. He means them to see Jesus as the Messiah, the Son of David (Matthew 1:1b); to realize that when they hear Jesus, they hear the voice of God and should, therefore, have no apprehension about his teaching, even if it calls for a change from what they've always known.

Reflect

If you knew nothing else about Jesus, what would convince you of his divinity? His Incarnation? His preaching? His Resurrection? Something else?

Pray

Lord, show me how to face change in my life with confidence and optimism rather than uneasiness and worry.

• • • | • • •

"Obey My Voice and I Will Be Your God"

March 31 • Third Thursday of Lent
Jeremiah 7:23–28; Luke 11:14–23

In Jesus' prologue to his lesson on the Law yesterday, he asked his audience (and us by extension) to understand an important lesson. Jesus says that living out God's ordinances in a certain manner, just because it is the way we've always done it, is both unproductive and disrespectful of God. God urges us to move out of our long-occupied comfort zones and set our feet in new directions.

We hear much the same message from Jeremiah who conveys God's grievance this way, "Thus says the LORD of hosts, the God of Israel: …For on the day that I brought your ancestors out of the land of Egypt, I did not speak to them or command them concerning burnt-offerings and sacrifices. But this command I gave them, 'Obey my voice, and I will be your God, and you shall be my people; and walk only in the way that I command you, so that it may be well with you'" (7:21, 22–23).

The point for God's people now as it was for God's people then is that outward religious acts and external piety are empty gestures when the hearts of the people do not accompany them. Through Jeremiah, God reminds the people of Judah that their ancestors were never asked to place their trust in rites and rituals, but rather to "obey my voice."

Reflect

This is not a new message. We've been hearing it off and on all through Lent. The question is: How does it apply to your personal spirituality and that of your parish community? For each person, the answer will be different.

Pray

Clear my vision, O Eternal One, so that I may recognize that even the most beautiful liturgies exist only to assist me in hearing and obeying you in all I do. Deliver me from going through the motions because this is the way we've always done it.

• • • | • • •

"Hear, O Israel!"
April 1 • Third Friday of Lent
Hosea 14:2–10; Mark 12:28–34

In a continuation of yesterday's premise, Hosea urges his people to return to their God, "for you have stumbled because of your iniquity." He is dealing with unrighteousness on a broad scale.

Jesus, on the other hand, encounters a single scribe who seemingly seeks righteousness. When he asks Jesus, "Which commandment is the first of all?" Jesus tells him, in effect, that he's fully capable of answering his own question, citing the Shema prayed daily by observant Jews. "Hear, O Israel, the Lord our God, the Lord is one; you shall love the Lord your God with all your heart, and with all your soul, and with all your mind, and with all your strength." Then he adds, "The second is this, 'You shall love your neighbor as yourself.'" These two commands are as old as the Judaic tradition itself.

During Lent, it is natural to look for new approaches, unique or exotic spiritualities. What Jesus might tell us is that we already know what we need to do; it's simply a matter of putting it into practice as Hosea today and Jeremiah yesterday counseled their people. Actually, we've come full circle back to the Ash Wednesday reading from the prophet Joel:

> Return to the LORD, your God,
> for he is gracious and merciful,
> slow to anger, and abounding in steadfast love,
> and relents from punishing. (Joel 2:13b)

Like the scribe, we have no need to be told anything new, unusual, or arduous. Jesus has already told us everything we need to know.

Reflect

The old *Baltimore Catechism,* for all its faults, began with one basic premise. We were made to know, love, and serve God in this life and be happy with him in the next. Knowing, loving, and serving follow logically one upon the next. Lent provides an extraordinary opportunity to consider how they play out in our lives.

Pray

Great teacher, keep telling me what I've known all along and show me how to implement your teaching in my life in a more effective and affective manner.

• • • | • • •

Holier Than Who?

April 2 • Third Saturday of Lent
Hosea 6:1–6; Luke 18:9–14

When we hear a person referred to as "holier than thou," it is generally not meant as a compliment. Instead, it implies someone who seems to believe he or she is more pious or closer to God than others. Additionally, and more negatively, it surmises that this attitude is completely unwarranted. That's the situation in today's parable.

The two men couldn't be more opposite: the Pharisee held in high esteem by the public and the tax collector held in practically no esteem whatsoever. And yet, as is often the case in Jesus' parables, it is the implausible party who comes out on top. Think how frequently tax collectors win the day in the Gospels. Matthew, chosen as one of the twelve, was a tax collector. Zacchaeus, who climbed a tree to see Jesus, was a tax collector. Jesus was upbraided for eating with tax collectors and sinners. So what made the tax collector in today's story so righteous? In a word, humility. He didn't think of himself as anything special. Quite the contrary: He threw himself without hesitation on the mercy of God.

Even their physical stances say something about the two men, the Pharisee "standing by himself" and the tax collector "standing far off." One considered himself too good to mix with the crowd; the other saw himself as too sinful to come any closer to the Holy of Holies. Again, as we've seen so many times thus far in Lent, it's a matter of attitude. God considers the heart, and behaving in a holier-than-thou manner is completely pointless and hollow.

Reflect
Don't get the wrong idea about humility. As Sister Joan Chittister, O.S.B., once wrote, "Humility is the ability to recognize my right place in the universe, both dust and glory."

Pray
Deliver me, my God, from an inferiority complex on the one hand or a superiority complex on the other. When

tempted to either, let me remember your attitude toward Pharisees and tax collectors.

• • • | • • •

Light Versus Darkness in So Many Ways

April 3 • Fourth Sunday of Lent

1 Samuel 16:1b, 6–7, 10–13a; Ephesians 5:8–14; John 9:1–41

Remembering that episodes in the Gospel of John often contain several layers of meaning, the story of the man born blind may be his masterpiece. As you read it, try to think of the many ways we are often blind to God in our lives.

In a repeat of yesterday's premise, we find a man, very ordinary even if blind, pitted against the highly respected Pharisees. The man is blind physically and evidently spiritually as well, while the Pharisees believe that they see everything clearly. Like the Samaritan woman in last Sunday's Gospel, the blind man comes gradually to the light, the knowledge of who Jesus really is. Initially, replying to a question as to the identity of his healer, he simply says, "the man called Jesus." Later he tells the Pharisees, "He is a prophet." Still later, after Jesus reveals himself, the man says with reverence, "Lord, I believe."

Meanwhile, the Pharisees who think themselves fully in the light are plunging into the darkness. Jesus calls them on it, and they sputter, "'Surely we are not blind, are we?' Jesus says to them, 'If you were blind, you would not have sin. But now that you say, "We see," your sin remains.'" It's almost like two elevators passing one another, one moving up toward the light and faith; the other descending into darkness.

John's characters typically move slowly but surely toward faith, toward being altogether in the light of faith in Jesus. Aren't we a lot like that, taking measured, tentative steps forward and, perhaps upon occasion, one step back? Like the blind man and the Samaritan woman, direction may be more important than speed.

Reflect

For most of us, a complete faith does not fall on us like a bolt from the blue. It builds step by step, little by little, over the months and years of our lives. A spiritual mentor of mine urged me to pray persistently for an increase in faith, and I do.

Pray

Jesus, heal my blindness as you healed the man in today's Gospel. I pray for an unceasing increase in my faith. Let me not lose hope should I stumble backward toward the darkness, but keep my eyes on the light that never fails.

• • • | • • •

The Signs All Point to Jesus
April 4 • Fourth Monday of Lent
ISAIAH 65:17–21; JOHN 4:43–54

After spending two days in Sychar where he had spoken with the Samaritan woman and other townspeople, Jesus moves north into Galilee (Samaria was located between Judea and Galilee) and the city of Cana, where he encounters a royal official whose son lies ill some distance away in Capernaum. Although we are not specifically told, the official was in all probability Roman, but that doesn't seem to enter into Jesus' decision to grant his request for a cure; only the man's confident trust counts.

Notice that the healing transpired at 1:00 PM which, in John, implies that the light was brightest and strongest: Jesus, the Light of the world. Take note as well of the final verse of the reading, "Now this was the second sign that Jesus did after coming from Judea to Galilee." John never refers to Jesus' wondrous works as miracles, but as signs. Signs, as we know, have little significance in themselves but point beyond to something of greater consequence. In this case, we are meant to focus on what Jesus does less than on who Jesus is. His signs point to his divinity. Would the royal official have gotten that message? Probably not, but Jesus is teaching his disciples the most valuable lesson of all: There is something more than a mere man here; there is God incarnate.

Reflect
Who is Jesus really, and what does that mean in our lives? This is a question we should keep asking ourselves throughout our lives. The answer could develop and intensify as the years pass.

Pray
Jesus, may I know you more profoundly, love you more passionately, serve you more single-heartedly, each day that I live.

· · · | · · ·
Living Water

April 5 • Fourth Tuesday of Lent
EZEKIEL 47:1–9, 12; JOHN 5:1–16

If asked to name the most valuable commodity in the Middle East, most would respond oil, but that is very wide of the mark. That commodity today remains what it has been since the dawn of time: water. Biblical pages are so full of water references, analogies, stories, poems, and allegories it's a wonder the pages aren't damp! And living water, which runs free as opposed to that stored for long periods in cisterns, was and is most precious of all.

Today, Ezekiel uses apocalyptic language to describe a river of life flowing in such luxuriant quantity that it all but engulfs him. This great stream emanates from the temple, the house of God, bringing life to everything it surges around. Such a stream also springs from the house of God that awaits us at the end of our earthly lives.

Jesus, too, is at the water's edge today where "lay many invalids—blind, lame, and paralyzed," hoping to be placed in the pool "when the water is stirred up." The pool was, in fact, one of many natural springs where underground movement sometimes made the waters swirl. This was considered to have healing power. On this day, it was not the water, but Jesus, who brought healing, a deed praiseworthy in the eyes of some onlookers, but blameworthy in the eyes of others because the healing took place on the Sabbath, a day hemmed in by hundreds of restrictions against what might be considered work on the Sabbath. Jesus seems to be saying, "Priorities, folks! Priorities!" His refusal to water down his message would prove costly in the end.

Reflect

Lent is a season ideally suited to reordering priorities or, at least, checking to see that they are already in the proper order. It's easy to let life rearrange what's important in our lives without our even noticing it.

Pray

Most of us sign ourselves with holy water upon entering a church. The next time you do that, make it a conscious prayer of awareness of the commitments made when the waters of baptism washed over you. You will be asked to renew those promises at the Easter Vigil.

• • • | • • •

Not Merely Confession But Reconciliation

April 6 • Fourth Wednesday of Lent
ISAIAH 49:8–15; JOHN 5:17–30

Contrary to popular belief, the role of the prophet is not primarily to foretell the future. Simply put, the prophet speaks for God. His message may have to do with the past, the present, or, yes, the future, but he is not a fortune-teller. So here, as in countless other sections of the prophetic books, Isaiah's words are prefaced by, "Thus says the Lord." It is then God who speaks:

> In a time of favor I have answered you,
>   on a day of salvation I have helped you;
>
> …
>
> For the LORD has comforted his people,
>   and will have compassion on his suffering ones.
> (49:8, 13)

How many people continue to carry tiring and tedious burdens of guilt over events long past? How many miserable souls believe their offense to be so unspeakable that God could never forgive them? That's not the message we're hearing this week, nor has it ever been. Lent provides an exceptional opportunity to assess the current state of our lives, that's true. But having done that, we are asked only to acknowledge where we missed the mark (which is what the word *sin* really means), confess that it was our own fault, make a determined resolution not to go down that road again, and move on. Leave that burden behind and move ahead as a free person beloved by God.

Keep an eye open for an opportunity to avail yourself of one of our faith's most glorious gifts, the sacrament of reconciliation…not merely confession nor penance, but reconciliation: "I will not forget you," says the Lord.

Reflect

Our reflection today might take the form of what has traditionally been called an examination of conscience in preparation for our formal reconciliation with a God who seeks not to punish, but to embrace.

Pray

During this blessed season, loving God, recall to my consciousness the many ways and times I have missed the mark. Let me take these into your sacramental presence, receive your forgiveness, and move on.

• • • | • • •

Where Would We Find a Golden Calf Today?

April 7 • Fourth Thursday of Lent
EXODUS 32:7–14; JOHN 5:31–47

Lest we be lulled into a false complacency by the readings earlier this week, today's passages deliver more sobering thoughts. While we should always depend on God's unconditional love for us, we should also be wary of presumption. "Do not be deceived; God is not mocked, for you reap whatever you sow," cautions Paul (Galatians 6:7). Our commitment to Christ, our allegiance to God, must be genuine, and our lives must steadfastly reflect that.

Not long before today's episode, "Moses came and told the people all the words of the Lord and all the ordinances; and all the people answered with one voice, and said, 'All the words that the Lord has spoken we will do'" (Exodus 24:3). Yet, merely because Moses was detained on the mountain of God, the same people were in short order worshipping a golden calf. Making promises and living them out are two distinctly different things.

Jesus reproved the people of Judah over a thousand years later for much the same shallow faith. Rejoicing for a while in the light of John the Baptist, they were nonetheless unwilling to believe in the one to whom John's preaching pointed.

Do we resolutely lean into the wind, refusing to allow our faith to be swayed, or are we blown about by every random gust, chasing one metaphorical golden calf after another?

Reflect

Today's readings are ideally suited to the lenten season when we step aside from our everyday lives to reexamine our promises to God, both those made at baptism and those we have personally entered into since.

Pray

Lord, keep me alert for potential golden calves in my life. Anything that has the capability of taking your rightful place in my heart is a false idol to be avoided at all costs.

• • • | • • •

A Dark Undertone in a Festive Time
April 8 • Fourth Friday of Lent
WISDOM 2:1A, 12–22; JOHN 7:1–2, 10, 25–30

The Feast of Booths or Tabernacles in Jesus' time was a joyous event that lasted for nine days. In addition to being a harvest festival of thanksgiving, it had historical significance, commemorating the long journey of the Israelites from Egypt to the Promised Land. You would, therefore, expect everyone to be in fine fettle, ready to enjoy a communal celebration.

Still, Jesus' appearance stirs some uneasiness in the crowd: "Is not this the man whom they are trying to kill? And here he is, speaking openly, but they say nothing to him! Can it be that the authorities really know that this is the Messiah?" (John 7:25–27)

Jesus, however, is not deceived by this short reprieve. Indeed, his enemies try without success to arrest him even as he preaches in the temple precincts. This is relatively early in John's Gospel, but even at this juncture, Jesus is aware that someday in Jerusalem these adversaries will arrest, torture, and kill him. Such a fate deters him not at all for he knows, even now, that death never has the last word; life always does.

The Christian understanding that life once created never ends is one of our most distinguishing traits, one of the qualities that makes us stand out from the crowd. And the crowd doesn't like that much as today's readings point out, especially the selection from the book of Wisdom. Wisdom, written less than a century before

Jesus' birth, seems to presage his lot. Death lies ahead for all of us. No exceptions will be made. But Jesus' own life-death-LIFE demonstrates forcefully that it is nothing to fear.

Reflect

Many notable biblical figures, like Jeremiah, the person described in Wisdom, and certainly Jesus, were challenged and hounded for their beliefs. How do you think you would respond under similar circumstances?

Pray

How can I thank you enough for the gift of life, my God? Every other gift stems from that, and just as you never withdraw any gift you bestow on me, I know you will never take back the gift of life. Life Is ForEver!

• • • | • • •

The Mood Darkens

April 9 • Fourth Saturday of Lent
JEREMIAH 11:18–20; JOHN 7:40–53

Ominous clouds continue to gather overhead as each day's readings bring us closer to the culminating events in the life of Jesus and our own. There don't seem to be many positive signs pointing to sunnier days ahead. It is often here that devoted Christians lose heart and lose sight of the Resurrection that lies beyond any fate that the cruelest of deaths can impose.

> But I was like a gentle lamb led to the slaughter.
> And I did not know it was against me
>   that they devised schemes…. (Jeremiah 11:19)

The degree of animosity around him may have taken Jeremiah by surprise, but it can hardly have been news to Jesus. The buzz was all around him. Who is this man? A much-anticipated prophet like Moses (Deuteronomy 18:18)? The long-awaited Messiah, the Anointed One of Israel? The descendant of the great king David who would restore the nation? An incomparable wonder-worker? All of the above? None of the above? Many saw him in a far harsher light—as a troublemaker, rabble-rouser, and fraud.

Who is Jesus really? As we mentioned earlier in these reflections, ultimately all faith issues for Christians hang on that single question. How each of us answers it will in large part determine the direction of our lives: what we value, how we love, why we live as we do.

Reflect

It didn't merely fall to the crowds in John's Gospel to grapple with Jesus' identity. It falls to you and me and is the one question we all must answer before our journey ends.

Pray

I cannot hope to know you, Jesus, unless you yourself allow it. Nor can I love or serve you as I wish without that knowledge. Please, allow me to know you just a little.

• • • | • • •

The Man Who Died Twice

April 10 • Fifth Sunday of Lent
EZEKIEL 37:12–14; ROMANS 8:8–11; JOHN 11:1–45

Belief in an afterlife and what it might entail developed little by little over many centuries. In today's short reading from Ezekiel, who lived some six centuries before Jesus, we have one of the earliest allusions to the resurrection of the body. By Jesus' time, this idea was held by some Jews but not others.

Martha clearly believes in this resurrection, probably due to her close friendship with Jesus and listening to him preach. "I know that he [Lazarus] will rise again in the resurrection on the last day" (John 11:24). Nonetheless, it seems more important to Jesus that she understand clearly that the power of life and death lay with him, "I am the resurrection and the life. Those who believe in me, even though they die, will live…" (John 11:25). Remember, at this point in the story, Martha has no sense of what Jesus is about to do, but she expresses her firm faith, "Yes, Lord, I believe that you are the Messiah, the Son of God, the one coming into the world" (John 11:27).

Still, she must have been dumbstruck when her brother emerged from his tomb. The raising of Lazarus would seal Jesus' doom with the religious hierarchy. "So from that day on they planned to put him to death" (John 11:53). We must remember that what Lazarus experienced was not resurrection, but resuscitation. He had to die again at some future date. Jesus, on the other hand, will not many days later come out of his tomb transformed as we will be upon our own resurrection.

As we draw closer to observing the tragic events of Jesus' passion and death, we must never lose sight of the light on the horizon, signaling the resurrection.

Reflect

Martha comes across in Scripture as a thoroughly pragmatic woman who might not be easily convinced. Yet, her statement of faith is unequivocal. If Jesus stood before us and asked us, as he asked Martha, "Do you believe this?" what would we say?

Pray

When those I love die, Lord, like Martha, I grieve. That's normal, natural, necessary. But let me never despair, secure in your words that you are the resurrection and the life, and those who believe in you, even though they die, will live.

• • • | • • •
Two Women, Two Different Verdicts
April 11 • Fifth Monday of Lent
Daniel 13:1–9, 15–17, 19–30, 33–62; John 8:1–11

Today, we are presented with two similar stories which have very different outcomes. In the first reading, a young woman named Susannah is accused of adultery although she is undeniably innocent. In the Gospel we encounter another woman accused of adultery, and this time she is unquestionably guilty. Both women must have been terrified, as the penalty for adultery was stoning, a horrible way to die. Neither expects mercy, as women had little recourse to defense in that culture.

Now let's turn our attention to those whose judgment will determine their fate. Poor Susannah has the misfortune of having as her accusers respected elders whose supposed wisdom would also be sought in arbitrating the case. They are perfectly willing to allow the false accusation to stand and the execution to take place. The woman in the Gospel is brought before Jesus by Pharisees and scribes of similar respectability. Although her guilt is clear, Jesus dismisses her with the mild admonition to, "Go your way, and from now on, do not sin again" (John 8:11).

Daniel rescues Susannah even as she is led away to execution by citing Jewish law, which seems to have been conveniently forgotten. Jesus silences the other woman's accusers by citing their own sinfulness. In both stories, we learn once again the futility, and in the case of Susannah the evil, of judging others. Jesus might say to us the same thing he said to the woman before him, "Go your way, and from now on, do not sin again."

Reflect

The accounts of these two women may bring to mind Jesus' comment about casting the log out of one's own eye before pointing to the splinter in someone else's. There's a good deal of lenten meditation material there.

Pray

Lord Jesus, like the woman in the Gospel, I stand before you sinful and sorrowful. I stand silently as she did, awaiting your judgment, bereft of excuses and completely dependent on a mercy I do not deserve.

• • • | • • •

Where Is Heaven?

April 12 • Fifth Tuesday of Lent
Numbers 21:4–9; John 8:21–30

An otherworldly quality surrounds today's readings. Jesus speaks of going away and of being from above while humanity remains earthbound. Moses, too, is seen crafting a serpent and placing it on a pole, requiring people to look up at it. Even the Responsorial Psalm tells of God looking "...down from his holy height; / from heaven he beheld the earth...."

Our vision, however, can be woefully restrictive, penning us into imagery that has long outlived its usefulness. Believing the earth to be a flat plate surmounted by an actual dome, our ancestors lived in a world that was almost always either horizontal or vertical, seldom angular, and almost never circular. Above the dome (the firmament) lived God. Conceptions of the universe in the twenty-first century bear little, if any, resemblance to ancient cosmology. Yet we still think of heaven as being up and of God looking down.

If it's only imagery, what does it matter what we think? It matters a great deal because it affects our understanding of our ultimate destiny with God. Because we will inhabit a realm where time and space are no longer factors, we lack a frame of reference. We can dream of what such a future might hold, as long as we don't allow ourselves to get hung up on notions of harps, clouds, halos, and pearly gates. Such fancies will no doubt prove to be pretty silly once we possess the real thing.

Reflect

We believe God to be everywhere. What does that do to your concept of heaven?

Pray

Lord, I can but echo the words of the apostle Paul:

> What no eye has seen, nor ear heard,
>   nor the human heart conceived,
> what God has prepared for those who love him.
> (1 Corinthians 2:9)

• • • | • • •

Choose!
April 13 • Fifth Wednesday of Lent
DANIEL 3:14–20, 91–92, 95; JOHN 8:31–42

As the decisive events of the coming week approach, the daily Scripture readings grow more insistent. The word *choose* resonates in our ears. Choose your path. If you elect to stay on Jesus' road, the miles ahead will test you sorely. If you seek a detour that offers easier going, it may turn into the ultimate deception. The seeds of intense suffering are contained within our preference. If not, why would one alternative be preferable to another?

The three young men the book of Daniel brings to our attention today are only too well aware that their refusal to obey the king of what was then the great superpower, Babylon, would almost inevitably result in consequences of the most unpleasant sort. But we hear them affirm, "If our God whom we serve is able to deliver us from the furnace of blazing fire and out of your hand, O king, let him deliver us. But if not, be it known to you, O king, that we will not serve your gods" (Daniel 3:17–18). Their decision was immovable, and they faced the fire with firm resolution.

Jesus sought just such faith from those who should have been most willing to confer it, the people who had for long centuries been covenanted to God. "If you continue in my word, you are truly my disciples…" (John 8:31). Their response must have been disappointing, "We are descendants of Abraham and have never been slaves to anyone." We are not told where their choice took them.

Reflect
Because God has given us free will, life is all about choice. We are the only creatures who have the capability of turning our backs on God and walking away. These coming days offer an unusual opportunity to examine the choices we're making.

Pray
I choose you, Lord, and I choose to follow. Following doesn't come easily to an independent American. I'll

need lessons and a considerable amount of patience on your part.

• • • | • • •

Ours Is a Noble Heritage
April 14 • Fifth Thursday of Lent
GENESIS 17:3–9; JOHN 8:51–59

With the exception of Moses, Abraham is the most revered figure in the Hebrew Scriptures, and the reason for that is apparent in today's reading from Genesis. Here, God enters into a remarkable covenant with this man. "I will establish my covenant between me and you, and your offspring after you throughout their generations, for an everlasting covenant…" (Genesis 17:7). All three major Near Eastern religions—Judaism, Christianity, and Islam—look upon Abraham as their foundational figure. But Abraham is not the founder for, as the verse above asserts, God took the initiative.

Abraham is concerned about two primary issues, heirs and land. He is assured that he will be "…the ancestor of a multitude of nations." Among those descendants will be Jesus…and us! Everyone covenanted to God in baptism is an heir to Abraham, if not genetically, spiritually.

Now Abraham lived some eighteen hundred years before Jesus; yet Jesus tells his critics, "…before Abraham was, I am," words that recall God's response to Moses at the burning bush. In those five simple words, Jesus declares his divinity. He is the man from Nazareth, yes, but so much more. He is also the Christ who has existed for all eternity: God incarnate; God divine; son of Abraham; Son of God. We, in turn, are children of Abraham and children of God. How well do we wear our noble heritage?

Reflect
When you think about people in the Bible, do they just seem like characters in a novel, or do you see some relationship with them? We are all part of the one family of God.

Pray
Lord, every time I make the Sign of the Cross and when I renew my baptismal vows at the Easter Vigil, remind me that I, like Abraham, am covenanted to you now and for all eternity.

Calm in the Face of Hatred

April 15 • Fifth Friday of Lent
JEREMIAH 20:10–13; JOHN 10:31–42

By now, the theme of the persecution of the righteous person is very familiar to us. It's easy to see Jesus in the reading from Jeremiah although nearly six centuries lie between them. One line from Jeremiah sums up the situation for both men, "Terror is all around!" What I find most impressive in both passages is their calm composure, each trusting in God in the face of irrational rage. In a scenario reminiscent of his response to a hostile hometown crowd (Luke 4:30), Jesus simply walks away from his adversaries. No recriminations. No shouting matches. Just a serene refusal to be drawn into the maelstrom of hatred.

Jesus evenly reveals, "…the Father is in me and I am in the Father…" (John 10:38). Blasphemy indeed if not true, but if true? Jeremiah prays:

> O LORD of hosts, you test the righteous,
>   you see the heart and the mind;
> let me see your retribution upon them,
>   for to you I have committed my cause.
> (Jeremiah 20:12)

Neither the Messiah nor the prophet ever takes his eyes off God. Like the three young men in the book of Daniel we read about on Wednesday, both Jesus and Jeremiah put their faith completely in God.

When we face opposition or downright anger, our first impulse is to fight back, verbally at the very least. What would happen if we listened to our adversaries and then coolly walked away without dignifying their accusations with a response? What if we simply put the situation in the hands of God and refused to allow the wrong to consume us? We might live far more peaceful lives.

Reflect
What we have in today's Gospel is another of Jesus' lessons in turning the other cheek. Have you ever been the victim of malicious injustice? If so, how did you respond?

Pray
When accusations against me are unmerited, abused Jesus, cool my wrath and help me to emulate you by walking away with a tranquil heart.

• • • | • • •
Gladness Versus Gloom
April 16 • Fifth Saturday of Lent
Ezekiel 37:21–28; John 11:45–56

The readings seem to present diametric opposites today. Ezekiel is full of joy; John, full of impending disaster. Ezekiel is the prophet of the Exile, the low point in Israel's history. Today, he tells the banished Israelites that they will leave Babylon and return to Jerusalem. Perhaps not immediately, but in due time, their sadness will be turned to elation.

For his part, Jesus enjoys a certain amount of adulation after the raising of Lazarus, but that will be short-lived in light of his enemies' growing resolve. "So from that day on they planned to put him to death. …Jesus therefore no longer walked about openly among the Jews…" (John 11:53–54). It should be noted, and emphatically, that Jesus, himself an observant Jew, never condemned all the Jews of his day and certainly not those of our own. His quarrel was with certain religious leaders. The shameful history of Christians who persecuted their spiritual ancestors is heartbreaking, and only recently have those hearts begun to open to one another again.

In Lazarus' return to life, Jesus surely sees a fore-shadowing of his own with the one remarkable difference we cited earlier. Lazarus, like all those Jesus raised from the dead, must die again. When Jesus rises, however, "...death no longer has dominion over him" (Romans 6:9b). He rises to new and eternal life. As his disciples, we shall follow him into that life. Pure gladness! No gloom! Little wonder, then, that Christians can never despair.

Reflect

Gladness and gloom play across our lives like sunshine and shadow. The Israelites certainly experienced both during and after the Exile. Like them, we are buoyed by the certainty that God never breaks his covenant with us. Sunshine will win out in the end.

Pray

Lord, you told Lazarus to come out. When you say those words to me, you will summon me to new life in a glorified body, to a life that will never end. How is it possible to thank you for such a gift?

• • • | • • •
Jesus Christ Is Lord!

April 17 • Palm Sunday of the Lord's Passion
MATTHEW 21:1–11; ISAIAH 50:4–7; PHILIPPIANS 2:6–11;
MATTHEW 26:14—27:66

Years ago, I attended a national convention which concluded with all attendees assembled for an impressive liturgy. Today's passage from Philippians was read, and as the lector intoned, "Jesus Christ is Lord," an enormous banner inscribed with those words was unfurled from a balcony above. I'll never forget it. It summed up neatly the essential reason all of us were gathered there, and it seems a fitting opening for the holiest week of the year. This week, more than any other, is all about defining who Jesus is…not was, but is at this very moment across the universe and deep in every individual heart and soul.

In some parishes today, Matthew's version of Jesus' triumphal entrance into Jerusalem will be read during the procession immediately preceding Mass. Parishioners may wave palm branches as the liturgical ministers advance up the aisle. Since we already know how the story ends and that some of those who laid down palms before Jesus on Sunday called for his execution six days later, we may wonder at our own sincerity as we brandish our branches. Will we still hail Jesus as Lord on Friday as we do this Sunday? Is our faith and love genuine and heartfelt? We've been examining those issues all through Lent, and by now should have a fairly accurate idea of where we stand on Palm Sunday, on Good Friday, and on Easter. The week ahead will focus us as nothing else can on the core beliefs of Christianity.

Reflect

Try to squeeze a little more quiet time for contemplation into the busy days of this coming week. Even if it's only a minute or two, it can help keep you centered on the events of this sacred week.

Pray

During that quiet time suggested above, make "Jesus Christ is Lord" your mantra, your prayer.

Good Friends Badly Needed

April 18 • Monday of Holy Week
ISAIAH 42:1–7; JOHN 12:1–11

Holy Week starts off quietly enough. If you didn't know better, if you couldn't hear those ominous drumbeats in the distance, you'd think this was going to be a week pretty much like any other. Jesus leisurely walks the two miles from yesterday's celebration in Jerusalem to the village of Bethany, home of his friends Martha, Mary, and Lazarus. A feast is in preparation for the recently revived Lazarus, but Jesus seems to be in attendance more as close and cherished friend than as wonderworker. We get the impression he has been a guest in this house many times. Here he can relax and be himself. He's like one of the family.

Recalling that in John's Gospel events never take Jesus by surprise, it's reasonable to assume his need to surround himself with this kind of homey acceptance and domestic affection before his world begins to unravel. In the house of these old friends, he can make himself at home because he is.

Just as human as we are in everything but sin, Jesus will require every ounce of encouragement, assistance, and tender affection those around him can muster. Before the week is out, he will long for it, ache for it, reach for it, but it will not always be there. Basking in the warmth of this humble Bethany home he knows so well braces him for what lies only a few days ahead.

Reflect
Jesus should feel as at home with us as he did with Martha, Mary, and Lazarus. What can you do during his particular week to demonstrate that he is your nearest and dearest friend?

Pray
I, too, will have need of strength this week, beloved friend, Jesus. Let us be there for each other with encouragement and love every step of the way.

· · · | · · ·

Celestial Light Battles Malevolent Darkness

April 19 • Tuesday of Holy Week
Isaiah 49:1–6; John 13:21–33, 36–38

"I am the light of the world. Whoever follows me will never walk in darkness but will have the light of life" (John 8:12). On the evening of the Last Supper, Jesus' light encounters the epitome of darkness, betrayal by a close friend. Chronologically, the lectionary readings are somewhat ahead of actual happenings, but that's almost inevitable with so much to report.

Today's Gospel takes place in the darkness of early evening and figuratively presages the darkness of Judas's plan, a plan which John's omniscient Jesus knows full well. One can only imagine the tension as the two men lock eyes. "Do quickly what you are going to do. ...he immediately went out. And it was night" (John 13:27, 30). Never had the contrast between light and darkness been as evident as it is here. The darkness into which Judas plunges is far more spiritual than material. Finding his way back into the light will be challenging and difficult if, indeed, he ever does.

In the days ahead, Jesus, raised on the Law and the prophets, may take consolation in passages such as Isaiah's, "I [God] will give you as a light to the nations, / that my salvation may reach to the end of the earth" (Isaiah 49:6). At this juncture, it's hard to see much light dead ahead, but the prophet suggests that the light will win out in the end.

Reflect

There have been times in our own lives when it seemed that darkness would unavoidably win, when light was a mere glimmer if it could be discerned at all. If you are enmeshed in such a situation at present, turn the circumstances and your face toward the Light of the World. Remember, even Judas may have ultimately been saved.

Pray

No matter how impenetrable the darkness, keep my eyes firmly fixed on you, Jesus, the Light of the World. In you there is no darkness.

· · · | · · ·
Familiar Prayers in Troubled Times
April 20 • Wednesday of Holy Week
Isaiah 50:4–9a; Matthew 26:14–25

Today, we hear Matthew's version of the scene presented by John yesterday. Everyone, even eyewitnesses, sees events slightly differently, and it's interesting to compare the various Gospel versions of events to see what one writer might emphasize more than another, or which details appear in a single account only.

But of equal interest today is the First Reading, Isaiah's third servant song. It's so easy for us to place these words on Jesus' lips although we really have no idea who the prophet had in mind when he wrote them, and we may never know. It is possible, however, that these words really did find their way to Jesus' lips, or at least to his mind, as the rest of this week played out. As we have mentioned previously, Jesus, as an observant Jew, was raised on the Law, the prophets, and the psalms. That he would be familiar with this passage is not out of the question. After all, his plaintive cry from the cross, "My God, my God, why have you forsaken me?" is a direct quote from Psalm 22:1.

It's only natural in times of pain, anxiety, or stress to resort to that which we know so well. Anguish and sorrow don't lend themselves well to poetic composition. Catholics fall back on the prayers that have been part of their lives from childhood: the Our Father, Hail Mary, Glory Be, and so on. When we do, it's comforting to realize we're in good company.

Reflect

What prayers do you say most often? Why do they hold so much appeal?

Pray

Jesus, you taught your apostles how to pray, and you were yourself a man of prayer. Teach me how to pray in good times and bad, secure in the trust that you will always hear me.

• • • | • • •

The Body of Christ. Amen!

April 21 • Holy Thursday
EXODUS 12:1–8, 11–14; 1 CORINTHIANS 11:23–26; JOHN 13:1–15

With the celebration of the Mass of the Last Supper this evening, we begin the holiest triad of days on the Christian calendar, the Easter Triduum. We begin by commemorating the institution of the Eucharist. Although John does not mention this in his Last Supper narrative, probably believing he had sufficiently covered the subject in chapter six of his Gospel, we do read the oldest account in Scripture, Paul's writing to the Corinthians about the year 56, at least a decade before the first gospel was formed.

Regardless of the source, the initial celebration of Jesus' real Body and Blood in the Eucharist establishes one of Catholicism's most sacred tenets, one we cherish as the very core of our identity. We affirm that each time we receive Communion with a firm, "Amen!": Yes, we believe! Yes, we, too, are the body of Christ!

As is apparent from the Exodus reading, the Last Supper has long been associated with the hallowed seder meal at Passover. One reason for this is that many scholars believe the Last Supper to have been a seder. Another is that both feasts fall close to one another in the calendar. Passover began on Monday of this week.

Tragedy will rule the day tomorrow, but for today, let us remember the great gifts of God to us, whether with his people of the First Testament at Passover or with his people of the Second Testament at the Last Supper.

Reflect

Only John tells of the washing of the apostles' feet, a humble action replicated at the Mass of the Last Supper. A pastor once told me he had great difficulty recruiting volunteers to have their feet washed. I wonder why. What do you think?

Pray

O Lord, flood every cell of my body, every facet of my mind, the deepest reaches of my soul, the most intransigent parts of my will, the most unruly of my emotions, the most uncertain aspects of my faith with your eucharistic self.

• • • | • • •

Symbol or Reality?

April 22 • Good Friday

ISAIAH 52:13—53:12; HEBREWS 4:14–16, 5:7–9; JOHN 18:1—19:42

The cross has long been the symbol of Christianity, and since Christianity is today the world's dominant religion, the cross is seen everywhere: inside and outside our churches, on chains around our necks, and adorning all manner of religious objects. We routinely make the Sign of the Cross when we begin our personal prayers or communal liturgies. But has the symbol appropriated the reality?

Many of the crosses that we wear or see are quite beautiful. Their artistry may draw our admiration. Would we be horrified if someone pointed out that what we are really wearing is an emblem of possibly the most brutal form of execution ever devised?

The Jesus who hung on the cross that first Good Friday bore little resemblance to the strong man who walked many miles on Judea and Galilee's dusty roads. Like Isaiah's Suffering Servant, "...so marred was his appearance, beyond human semblance, and his form beyond that of mortals." He was in physical agony, emotionally spent, mentally and spiritually drained. Because crucifixion ultimately suffocated its victims, it would have taken every ounce of strength Jesus had to speak, so the few words the Gospel writers record take on deeper meaning. We would not wish such a death on the most heinous criminal, let alone the Son of God. And to think, all of this and so much more were endured out of love for us, each and every one of us. It's more than we can comprehend.

Reflect

If you are wearing a cross today, remove it, hold it in your hands, and contemplate what it represents.

Pray

Crucified Jesus, each day that I live, let me know you more profoundly, love you more passionately, serve you more single-heartedly.

• • • | • • •

And Now We Wait

April 23 • Holy Saturday

GENESIS 1:1—2:2; GENESIS 22:1–18; EXODUS 14:15—15:1;
ISAIAH 54:5–14; ISAIAH 55:1–11; BARUCH 3:9–15, 32—4:4;
EZEKIEL 36:16–17A, 18–28; ROMANS 6:3–11; MATTHEW 28:1–10

To keep vigil means to wait for something to happen. Some years ago, I kept vigil at my mother's bedside on the last night of her earthly life. I waited in the midnight quiet of the nursing home for that magical moment of transition into the life for which we are all born. It was an experience I'll never forget and wouldn't have missed. There was such a sense of hovering between this life and the next, I almost held my breath in expectation.

Tonight we keep vigil at Jesus' tomb, waiting for we know not what. Well, that's not exactly true because we know how the story turned out. Still, Holy Saturday has been described as the night Jesus went from tomb to womb. His sepulcher became the source of glorified new life. Mortals had never seen the like before and haven't since. It was a one-time happening that defines all of human history.

But before the Easter Vigil eucharistic liturgy springs to life with its glorious alleluias, we retrace salvation history from the first creation account in Genesis to the resuscitation of the dry bones in Ezekiel. As we listen, we remember how God's people finally arrived at this glorious night, how we got from the first microcosm of creation to the Resurrection of the Son of God. There exists no more awe-inspiring story. Finally, Paul tells the Romans, "[W]e will certainly be united with him in a resurrection like his." That's our future, yours and mine, he's talking about! And then there is Matthew's joyful account of Mary Magdalene and the other Mary discovering the empty tomb. Jesus has risen, and death no longer has dominion over him...or us. We are, indeed, Easter people, and alleluia is our song.

Reflect

As you sit in the darkened church tonight listening to the story of our faith, give some thought to the fact that Easter tells us death is a lie.

Pray

Almost giddy with joy and thrilled for those being baptized into you this holy night, O Risen Christ, the only prayer I can manage is Alleluia! Alleluia! Alleluia!

• • • | • • •

This Is the Day the Lord Has Made

April 24 • Easter Sunday

ACTS 10:34A, 37–43; COLOSSIANS 3:1–4 OR 1 CORINTHIANS 5–6B–8;
JOHN 20:1–9 OR MATTHEW 28:1–10; (EVENING) LUKE 24:13–35

"This is the day the Lord has made; / let us rejoice and be glad in it." Those words are taken from Psalm 118, today's responsorial, and never were words more apt. Psalm 118 is part of a set of psalms which form part of the seder ritual at Passover, so if the Last Supper was, as many scholars believe, a seder, this may well have been the last psalm Jesus sang before leaving for the Mount of Olives. The whole paschal mystery is there, the profound sorrow followed by the overwhelming joy.

Today is the greatest day of the Christian year, but it does not stand alone. Today marks the beginning of the seven weeks of Easter, a liturgical season longer than Advent, Lent, or Christmas. And that's not all. Each Sunday of the year is intended to be a little Easter which is why Sundays are never considered penitential and, therefore, not included in the days of Lent. We could reasonably sing today's response every weekend, "This is the day the Lord has made; / let us rejoice and be glad in it." The only addition we might consider making is: The Lord is risen indeed! Alleluia! Alleluia! Alleluia!

Reflect

Read Psalm 118 in its entirety, pausing to drink in verses 19–29 especially. Imagine those words on the lips of Jesus.

Pray

> You are my God, and I will give thanks to you;
>   you are my God, I will extol you.
>
> O give thanks to the LORD for he is good,
>   for his steadfast love endures forever.
> (Psalm 118:28–29)